STUDENT-GENERATED INDUCTION:
A SOCIAL IDENTITY APPROACH

A Staff Development Guide
NICHOLAS BOWSKILL

ACKNOWLEDGEMENTS

I am eternally grateful to my mum and dad, Hilda and Edward Bowskill. This book is also for my Auntie Norma who sadly passed away before this project was completed. Their love and support throughout my life is greatly appreciated.

I am equally indebted to my wife Linda and our two daughters Eleanor and Hannah. The time and love they gave me, to develop these ideas and write this guide, was invaluable.

This guide is a by-product from my doctoral research at University of Glasgow. As such, I am eternally grateful to Professor Vic Lally and to my other PhD supervisors – Quintin Cutts, Steve Brindley and Steve Draper. Thanks also to Sheena Banks and David McConnell as valued friends and colleagues.

Finally, I am indebted to Andrew Frain from the Australian National University, Canberra for his help in developing my theoretical thinking.

CONTENTS

1. Overview of the Pack..1

2. Orientation to Theory and Practice 7

3. Workshop Notes...19

4. The Workshop Script...29

5. The Workshop Slides..61

6. The Workshop Reading List...107

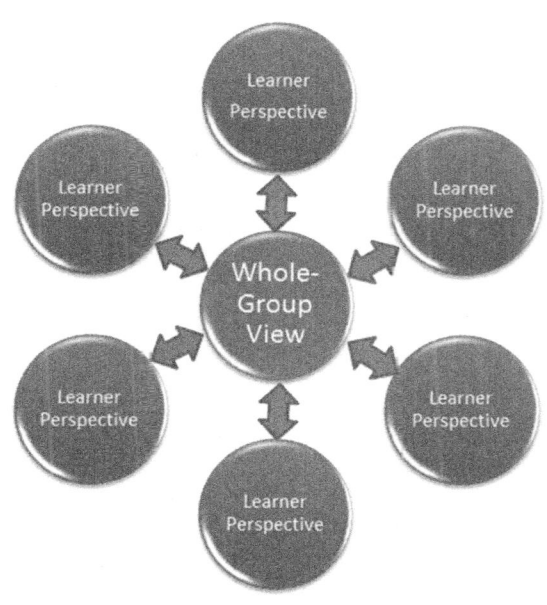

Part One:

OVERVIEW OF THE PACK

OVERVIEW OF THE GUIDE

KEY

SharedThinking is a technique that uses interactive technology in the classroom. It offers a way of learning together as a whole-group. It is distinct from the design of learning based on a representative individual. We have developed many different variations of the basic approach. The technique is described in more detail later in this guide.

Student-Generated Induction is one application of the SharedThinking technique. This application extends to include student-generated transition.

Social Identity Theory is a theoretical framework used to explain how the Shared-Thinking technique works as a relational approach to learning. It is used in this guide to explain how engagement, togetherness and belonging form part of student-generated induction.

Aims of the Guide

This guide is aimed at those in a staff development role who may be interested or involved in student induction/transition. Specifically, it is likely to be of value to those in student services, staff development and information professionals. It may also appeal to learning technologists as well as academics and professionals in Human Resources.

These materials will help you deliver a workshop on student-generated induction. The workshop is an opportunity for participants to reflect on their provision. It is also an experiential approach that models the student-generated induction process.

The materials are designed for you to run the workshop as it stands. Equally, it should be clear enough for you to modify it. For instance, it is possible to extend the workshop in various ways. Selections from the readings can be used before or after a session. Pie-charts from other SharedThinking sessions can also be re-used. If you wish to run the complete workshop then it will take about one day.

The Structure of the Guide

There are four main parts to this guide. They are: Workshop Notes, Workshop Script, Workshop Slides and Workshop Resources. Each of these is described briefly below.

Workshop Notes

Under this heading, we provide you with the aims and objectives of the workshop. We outline the structure of the workshop, the goals and the rationale for each part. We also provide details of the resources required.

Workshop Script

For each part of the workshop, we provide a script. These are the words that could be used for a particular slide. The script should help you understand the idea behind each slide and the core message intended. We anticipate that people will want to make the workshop their own and adapt it. That could include adapting any given slide or changing the workshop as a whole. We are effectively providing you with a workshop template and the words that *could* be used straight off the shelf.

Workshop Slides

We provide the slides for each part of this workshop. They are supported by the scripts to accompany each slide. All the slides are numbered and those numbers correspond to the same number in the script.

These slides and the accompanying script have already been used in professional development workshops. These events were held at different institutions around the UK. This means you can have confidence that the workshop you might deliver will be successful.

This workshop relies upon the use of technologies, such as voting systems or interactive whiteboards. In order to deliver the student-generated induction approach described here, you will need to have both the presentation software and the voting software installed.

Workshop Resources

We provide you with pie-charts from different case studies where this approach has already been used for induction or transition. The pie-charts are available at: http://www.flickr.com/photos/sharedthinking and they can be used as you like. These pie-charts, and others you may generate, give you the chance to develop additional activities as part of the workshops.

Other optional activities include putting two different pie-charts together on one slide. This offers a basis for comparisons to be made between different groups, for example. Alternatively, these artifacts might be a learning resource to offer online. Participants can explore such resources alone or together. These additional activities can help to extend these discussions within and beyond the initial workshop.

In addition, we have also provided you with a short reading list. This list covers some of the core literature on student induction and also on social identity theory. This includes the originators of the theory who are Henri Tajfel and John Turner. Reference to Alex Haslam's work is also included. Haslam is acknowledged as influential in the development of some ideas to do with this workshop.

These readings can also serve different purposes. On the one hand, they can be a resource to help you become more knowledgeable about the theoretical framework used here. This can help prepare you to deliver the workshop. On the other hand, the readings can be used as a resource for the workshop participants. They could be used either before or after the workshop.

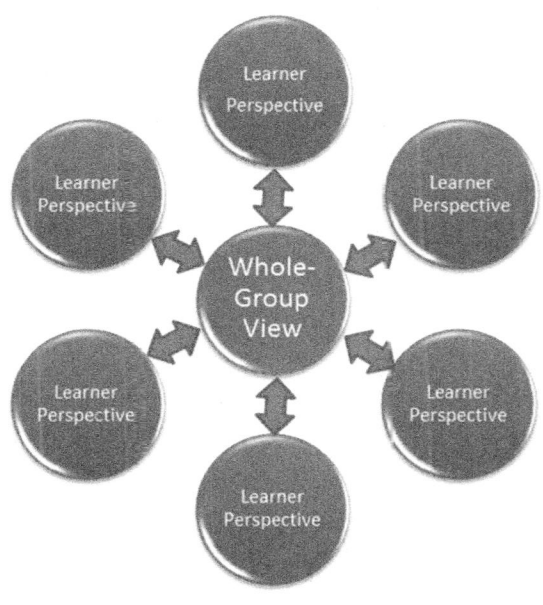

Part Two:

ORIENTATION TO THEORY AND PRACTICE

ORIENTATION TO THEORY AND PRACTICE

'Student-Generated Induction: A Social Identity Approach' is a phrase comprising of two parts. The term 'student-generated induction' is a pointer towards a social and participative idea of both induction and transition. This is in contrast to the popular idea of induction in which individuals, whilst sat in groups, are *told* what they need to know.

The *student-generated* aspect is also a reference to a specific and very concrete practice. We call this wider practice 'SharedThinking.' This practice supports those involved in bringing these social and participative principles to life, within the classroom or lecture theatre. It also offers a relational and highly-structured process for learning in large groups. 'Student-generated induction' is one of many applications of the SharedThinking practice.

'A social identity approach' is a reference to the theoretical framework that seeks to explain the design and implementation of the SharedThinking practice. The use of the word *approach* rather than *theory* is a reference to the wider view of social identity as a family of theories. That family includes Social Identity Theory, originated by Henri Tajfel (Tajfel 1969; Tajfel 1974) and Self-Categorization Theory originated by John Turner (Turner 1975; Turner 1991). Each of these researchers made a particular contribution to the theoretical project which constitutes 'the social identity approach.'

This theoretical work is largely centred within the discipline of social psychology. Student-generated induction and SharedThinking are innovations that draw upon and build on the work of these theorists. The outcome is a new social practice supported by classroom technology.

Technology and the SharedThinking Learning Design

At a practical level, SharedThinking is the combination of a snowball group discussion technique with the use of classroom technologies. Those technologies include electronic voting systems (clickers) and interactive whiteboards.

Structurally, this is a process that moves from an individual action to a whole-group activity (the snowball technique). The technology is used to allow individual and anonymous input. It is also a vehicle to capture and visualise the conversation in the classroom. The technology makes the snowball technique scalable and more efficient.

At a social and psychological level, SharedThinking can be understood as the co-construction of digital representations of the common ground within a particular group. These social representations (Moscovici 1988; Moscovici and Markova 1998) constitute the group-specific and context-sensitive social norms for the given group. You can think of these as ad-hoc social norms. Such representations give participants an opportunity to appreciate the *nature* of the group and its views on a particular matter.

Through identification, and co-authoring, the suggestion is that individuals will be prompted to compare their thoughts and feelings to those of the group (Livingstone, Haslam et al. 2011). This is fundamental to the relational and group-specific view of learning design made possible using the SharedThinking technique. This is a radical departure from a view of learning design based on representative individuals (instructional design).

By implication, we need to look beyond the individual for some sources of individual and group development. In this view of learning, groups are seen as having agency. The group view, co-generated by the SharedThinking process, functions as a resource for each individual.

A sampling of the literature on electronic voting systems showed that the most common use of this technology involves the tutor setting the questions *and* the options to be considered. SharedThinking is distinct in the way that participants co-construct the question options.

In this new approach, the facilitator frames the session with a question. That provides an initial orientation for the participants. The rest of the work is done by the group who create the options through dialogue and interaction. Each individual then votes to help visualise the collective view of those co-generated options.

The 'core' activity-structure (below) became identified as the SharedThinking technique. From that initial structure, we have since developed different variations and other applications. The core activity-structure is:

- Individuals write down their personal view on the topic-focus

- Move into small groups to share individual views

- Each group identifies one aspect to be recorded on the screen

- Create a set of question-options from the discussions

- Each individual votes on the aspect they see as most significant

- Voting generates a pie-chart on the public screen

- Plenary discussion on issues arising

This structure provided an initial *engine* for students to co-construct question-options. We have since scaled this up to accommodate over three hundred participants in a single induction session. We have further refined the technique to include the use of different classroom technologies such as interactive whiteboards and text messaging in class.

As such, the SharedThinking practice has been developed and implemented for a variety of different applications and audiences. This guide provides you with an initial introduction to one of those applications using the basic SharedThinking engine. That application is for student-generated induction (and transition).

The Workshop in the Context of Induction Design

By way of background to the workshop, and to help you make sense of the materials in the guide below, we offer the following overview:

   1. An individual view of induction

   2. A Structural view of induction

   3. An identity based view of induction

In what follows, we discuss three different ways of thinking about the design of student induction. This is intended to be a primer for you to help support the delivery of the workshop. It should help you understand the way that the workshop is organized. This may also be useful to give to workshop participants as a hand-out.

1. An Individual view of induction

It is possible to conjure an image of a representative individual and to base the design of your induction program around such a person. With that individual in mind, the task then becomes one of organizing the right content to be delivered in the optimal way for such a person to understand the institution. This is a popular approach to instructional design.

We can think of this as an approach to induction which is contained within the boundary of the individual mind (embodied). Following a *Piagetian* principle, the individual has the agency and the responsibility to process the information (Piaget and Inhelder 1969; Piaget 1977). That individual is seen as the only person that can modify their internal structures as they make sense of that new information. It is their responsibility to act on that information in ways appropriate to their perceived needs.

Induction providers can facilitate the acquisition process by aligning their messages to the appropriate level for that notional individual. However, only the individual is able to process that information in order to make it meaningful.

From this perspective, the design of induction can be understood as the provision of the information needed by a representative individual. That would be the information adequate to enable them to function within their new institutional environment.

A series of presentations, welcome guides, and other information are at the heart of this kind of provision. Socialization is typically addressed separately through events such as Fresher's Fairs and social events. Sports and social clubs are also seen as part of that informal socialization process.

2. A Structural View of Induction

Other theories recognize the social factors involved in learning. For instance, Social Constructivism locates agency, and some of the responsibility for learning, in the actions and thoughts of tutors (or more knowledgeable others). The ability to tune into a learner through dialogue and interaction might then increase the possibility of development beyond the level an individual might achieve alone (Vygotsky 1978).

From an induction perspective, this might suggest that presentations from tutors or support professionals could be useful in the overall design process. For example, students one year ahead on a course might be more able to understand and empathize with the situation of new arrivals. They may be more able to tune into their needs and feelings.

The richness of this, as a perspective-taking task, is still an issue at induction. The amount of information and the way in which it is presented to new arrivals can be challenging. Having just arrived, students might struggle to understand how these different presentations fit into their academic lives and which points are most important in the short-term.

Simpler and more relevant information may help the learner to process it (Thompson and Fine 1999). That information might otherwise appear too complex to be easily understood. This prompts us to think about induction as a task to organize the physical and informational environment in an optimal way. For example, we might decide to raise the profile of support services and make the students aware of the available resources and how to access them quickly and easily.

We could also arrange the electronic environment along similar lines. We might have pages on Facebook, websites, email alerts, and be on Twitter, as just some of the ways we might provide convenient, easily accessible information.

These are all ways in which a structural approach to induction and transition may be helpful. This is a view of the design of induction based on ways we organize people and information. Most importantly, this is a view of induction design which takes us beyond the boundaries of the individual mind.

3. An identity based view of induction

An alternative model is to think about the design of induction based upon identity. More precisely, we have designed a view of induction (and transition) based upon the development of *social* identity. This is applied to the group of new arrivals.

To understand this, we need to know what is meant by social identity. We also need to distinguish that from whatever may be meant by a *personal* identity.

We can describe personal identity as particular to a given individual. These are the ways in which we are each unique people. My personal identity is who I am. In contrast, a *social* identity is one that is not restricted to a given individual. It is an identity which others have as well.

Specifically, a social identity is the view we have of ourselves as members of a group. Our social identity is who we are as a group. The more obvious examples of social identities would be religion, ethnicity, gender, or sports teams. There are many others.

As Alex Haslam has pointed out, social identities are therefore organizers and coordinators of social interaction (Haslam, Eggins et al. 2003). In theory, we are able to work with other members of that identity-group via a shared perception of what constitutes group membership. Specifically, this is mediated by our perception of its social norms. In football, for example, each player would hold a view of what it means to be a footballer and they would interact accordingly.

Based on this theory, we would aim to organize a shared sense of group-identity in the mind of each individual. This would be done by jointly developing a shared understanding of what it means to be a new student arriving at their given institution. If we were also able to *visualise* the common ground, and facilitate social-identification, it is quite likely that each participant would relate their thoughts to those of the group (Livingstone, Haslam et al. 2011).

SharedThinking provides a technique for generating a sense of group-identity prompting *engagement* with the ad-hoc norms of our new group. When we see ourselves as *belonging* to a group, we become invested in the feelings, activities and ideas within that group. If successful, this interactive and dialogical technique should therefore induce an emotional sense of togetherness as the ad-hoc norms are co-constructed and then made visible. This sense of belonging should also support retention and well-being.

Here, we have a different basis for thinking about the design of learning as applied to induction and transition. It is a design approach which is based on a co-constructed sense of group membership and the joint-authoring of its ad-hoc norms.

Based on this social identity approach, we designed the SharedThinking practice. Student-generated induction is one particular application of this practice. This workshop and these materials should help you introduce and discuss this distinctive idea of induction with your participants.

Student – Generated Induction

This guide provides a workshop that models the practice of student-generated induction. Firstly, this is an approach in which students tell each other about their concerns. Secondly, this is an approach which communicates those concerns to staff. It is important to keep in mind that the primary aim of the process is to facilitate a conversation amongst the participants. This is in contrast with the more conventional notion of *telling* the students what we think they should know.

Of course, there will be information that students need and that will be unknown to them when they arrive. The student-generated approach to induction is mindful of the importance of any information gaps. It is organized to allow this to be added towards the end of the process. When the students have had an opportunity to share and discuss their immediate concerns they should be more ready to listen to additional information.

Dialogue and interaction are seen as a means of helping to reduce some of the initial anxieties that may be felt by students when they arrive at university. Providing a structured conversational approach allows them to voice their concerns. This also helps them appreciate that others share similar concerns. As such, this approach is as much to do with mental well-being as it is to do with informational needs.

As mentioned earlier, student-generated induction is a process supported by the use of classroom technologies. These include audience response systems (clickers) or interactive whiteboards. We have developed many variations of the standard approach used in this workshop. These include modifications to the structure as well as the re-use of artifacts from different sessions. Even so, this workshop should give you and your participants a useful grounding in both the theory and practice of this design approach.

This workshop aims to provide you with a framework and the resources necessary to implement an experiential workshop on student-generated induction and social identity theory. This staff development workshop has been tried and tested in several different settings. We found it worked well with groups of between twelve and forty staff in a typical workshop (the student-generated induction practice has been implemented with over three hundred students in a single session).

References:

Haslam, S. A., Eggins, R. A., & Reynolds, K. J. (2003). The ASPIRe model: Actualizing Social and Personal Identity Resources to enhance organizational outcomes. Journal of Occupational and Organizational Psychology, 76(1), 83-113.

House, J. S. (2001). Social Isolation Kills, But How and Why? Psychosomatic Medicine, 63(2), 273-274.

Livingstone, A. G., Haslam, S. A., Postmes, T., & Jetten, J. (2011). "We Are, Therefore We Should": Evidence That In-Group Identification Mediates the Acquisition of In-Group Norms. Journal of Applied Social Psychology, 41(8), 1857-1876. doi: 10.1111/j.1559-1816.2011.00794.x

Moscovici, S. (1988). Notes towards a description of Social Representations. European Journal of Social Psychology, 18(3), 211-250.

Moscovici, S., & Markova, I. (1998). Presenting Social Representations: A Conversation. Culture Psychology, 4(3), 371-410. doi: 10.1177/1354067x9800400305

Piaget, J. (1977). Problems of equilibration. In M. H. Appel & L. S. Goldberg (Eds.), Topics in cognitive development (pp. 3-14). New York: Plenum.

Piaget, J., & Inhelder, B. (1969). The Psychology of the child. New York: Basic Books, Inc.

Tajfel, H. (1969). Cognitive aspects of prejudice. Journal of Social Issues, 25, 79-97.

Tajfel, H. (1974). Social identity and intergroup behaviour. Social Sciences Information/Information sur les Sciences Sociales, 13, 65-93.

Thompson, L., & Fine, G. A. (1999). Socially shared cognition, affect, and behavior: a review and integration. Pers Soc Psychol Rev, 3(4), 278-302.

Turner, J. C. (1975). Social comparison and social identity: Some prospects for intergroup behaviour. European Journal of Social Psychology, 5(1), 1-34. doi: 10.1002/ejsp.2420050102

Turner, J. C. (1991). Social Influence. Milton Keynes: Open University Press.

Vygotsky, L. S. (1978). Mind in Society: The development of higher psychological processes. Cambridge, MA: Harvard University Press.

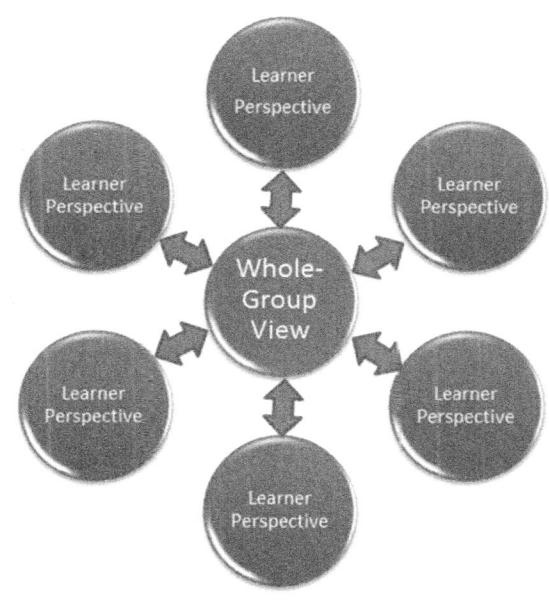

Part Three:

WORKSHOP NOTES

STUDENT-GENERATED INDUCTION WORKSHOP

Workshop Notes

These notes provide you with an overview of the aims, structure, and resources available for this workshop. We also provide guidance on the resources required to deliver this workshop.

Aims of this Workshop

The aim of the workshop is to facilitate a reflective discussion of current induction practices amongst a group of professionals. The parallel goal is to provide an experiential model of the student-generated induction/transition process already being used in different institutions.

To deliver this workshop you will require:

- A laptop computer

- Electronic voting software

- A receiver attached to the computer

- Enough voting handsets for one per participant

- Spare handset batteries

- A copy of PowerPoint presentation software

- A digital projector

- A screen

There are many different providers of electronic voting software. They each have different features. We do not distinguish between them here. Your institution may already have these resources or a preferred supplier. Check with your Audio Visual Department, learning technologists, or computer support staff for local recommendations and advice.

The Workshop in Brief

This workshop can be delivered in one day or it can be delivered in several chunks each of one to two hours' duration. This workshop is divided into a number of stages as follows:

1. Introduction to Social Identity Theory

Allow about twenty minutes for this section. This includes covering health and safety, the workshop structure, and the opening presentation.

This first section of the workshop is a presentation. This provides an overview of the aims of the workshop and its structure. It then introduces Tinto's theory of retention and his notion of developing learning communities in support of that theory (Tinto 1995; Tinto 2000). The workshop proposes the idea of groups and group membership as an alternative way of thinking about learning design for induction. This section goes on from there to discuss three alternatives for the design of induction. At the end of this section, the focus shifts to social identity as a new basis for designing induction and transition.

2. Technology Warm-Up

Allow about twenty minutes for this section. Please note you will need access to voting technology of some kind in order to deliver this and subsequent sections.

This section is important for two reasons. Firstly, you need to be certain that the technology is going to be reliable and that it is likely to function properly once the serious part of the workshop begins (in the next section). In addition, you also need to prepare the participants so that they feel comfortable with the technology and it does not become an obstacle to the flow of their conversations.

For this section, you will need to develop three general knowledge questions. These can often be developed from information generally available on the internet. We have left the slides blank with only the instruction to 'type option here.' One idea is to generate questions based on the local area in which you are holding the workshop. It could equally be useful to come up with questions to do with the particular institution or department. The aim is to make it both relevant and fun.

This is also a light moment after some new concepts were introduced in the opening presentation. It is also a shift from listening to participating. This section should also serve the participants as an ice-breaker.

3. Review of Concerns about Current Induction Practice

Allow about 30 minutes for this activity.

This section also serves two purposes. The first is to provide a structure and an opportunity for participants to share and discuss their concerns relating to their induction practice. The second purpose is the goal of using that discussion, and the activity-structure, as a way to model the basic form of student-generated induction and the basic SharedThinking practice.

4. Review of Positive Aspects of Current Induction practice

Allow about 30 minutes for this activity.

This section uses the same activity structure as in the previous activity/section. However, this time the technology is not used. Make sure you have a flipchart and pens available to write down the options from the different small groups and to record the votes.

Again, there are different purposes in this activity. One of the aims is to change the disposition of participants from the previous activity. Here they explore the positive aspects of their current practice. This should help them understand disposition-management as one of the tools of the SharedThinking practice. It may be useful to point out this affective dimension as one feature of this approach if you have chance.

The additional aim is to connect to the activity that follows this section. There you will be using these two activities as a basis for comparison. In the following activity participants will be invited to review the impact of technology in relation to the activity structure.

5. Exploration of the role of technology in classroom induction

Allow about fifteen minutes for this activity if you run it as a plenary review. Allow slightly longer if you decide to go back into small groups first.

This activity will only make sense if you have implemented the previous two activities. You should have used the same activity structure with and without technology by the time you come to do this activity.

The aim here is to invite participants to review the two preceding activities and identify the contribution made by the technology. In doing so, the idea is to create a reflective opportunity for the participants to consider the *process* distinct from the *content* of the session.

To make this activity easier for your participants, and to avoid becoming too much of a distraction from the wider aims of the workshop (to share current induction practices), a set of possible criteria can be provided on the slide. This option may help to stimulate and structure the reflective dialogue.

You should be aware that these are just a guide. Any or all of the given criteria can be set aside if desired. Running the activity without providing any prior criteria may make a greater demand upon some participants and for some that may be more rewarding. Your decision will be influenced by the time available and your knowledge of the participants.

6. *Exploring of concerns about diversity in induction*

Allow about thirty minutes for this section.

This activity also has a dual purpose. On the one hand, it is an opportunity to explore another induction-relevant issue which is how best to address the issue of diversity at induction. This should help to add further depth to the overall investigation of current induction practices as part of the workshop.

On the other hand, this activity links to the following section which discusses the way diversity can be understood within the theoretical context of the workshop. Specifically, we argue for a very fluid view of diversity. We can understand categories of diversity as social identities. This should help you set up the next section which elaborates upon the initial introduction to social identity theory given at the start of the workshop.

You should be careful to encourage the broadest view of diversity amongst your participants. This includes (and is not limited to): race, gender, ethnicity, sexuality, religion etc. as just some of the possible dimensions of diversity.

You should also be aware that for some people these can be difficult topics so be sensitive in your handling of this activity. Encourage an atmosphere of inquiry and mutual respect at all times. As a responsible professional, you should <u>always</u> challenge any form of discrimination should it arise.

7. More on social identity theory

Allow about twenty minutes for this section.

This section is another presentation and it seeks to deepen participants' theoretical knowledge. It follows on from, and should be explicitly connected to, the previous activity that explored the issue of diversity at induction.

The aim of this section of the workshop is to reconcile any potential conflict between a pluralist view of diversity and a possibly mono-cultural view which may be implied in Tinto's idea of developing a learning community. The theory argues for a context-sensitive view of identity.

This SharedThinking practice is to be understood as a process in which participants co-construct a shared sense of group-identity. Participants are co-authoring their group-specific social norms for the purpose of induction.

This simultaneously allows individual differences of identity to be sustained and developed in a way that is respected and unthreatened. The SharedThinking process seeks only to add the induction-group membership as another social identity. In this way, the presentation you provide in this section should connect with the previous activity in the workshop.

8. Concerns to do with using group-learning for Induction

Allow about 30 minutes for this activity.

This activity also has three different goals. The first of these is to allow participants an opportunity to share and discuss concerns they may have about the idea of adopting a collaborative approach to induction.

The second goal is, to use the discussion as an opportunity for participants to reflect upon the experience of the SharedThinking process in this workshop. The hope is that the workshop experience, as a collaborative approach, may be considered by participants as a possible solution to address some of their concerns about group-learning for induction.

The final goal here is strategic. The aim is to generate a resource for the next section's activity. That next section provides you with an opportunity to organise a comparison between different sessions and groups. This can be done when you place the pie-chart from this activity with one created elsewhere on the same issue.

9. Measures of student-generated induction

Allow about fifteen minutes for this section.

This section of the workshop is another presentation. The aim is to show how the Shared-Thinking process provides a means of sampling collective experience efficiently. It should also be stressed that this is a process of inquiry for both staff and students.

One option is to use the pie-charts generated in the previous section of the work-shop. This can be placed alongside products from a different session on the same topic. Note that additional pie-charts are available from the Flickr social media web site for this workshop. This is located at: http://flickr.com/photos/sharedthinking

As mentioned, this provides an opportunity for comparisons of the experience of one group with that of another. During the tea-break there should be an opportunity for you to organise this onto a single slide. Try and have the pie-chart from the other external session in place on your slide. That way you can copy and paste the pie-chart from this session alongside. This will enable your comparison.

If time does not allow, or you prefer to have this activity set up beforehand, then use pie-charts from two different external sessions. This may have different significance for the workshop group but it will show how it is possible to compare and contrast different collective experiences as a learning activity.

You have the opportunity to open up another discussion with your participants. This could be about the concerns and benefits of making such comparisons. It could be a conversation about using comparative views as part of induction and transition. It may also be an opportunity to ask your participants about the impact of seeing such views. This may give you an evaluative window on the impact of the workshop in general.

10. Review and Close

Allow about fifteen minutes for this final section.

This is an opportunity to recap on the activities in this workshop. We suggest this is done from the perspective of the participants as staff reviewing their practice (in other words, how useful it may have been as a vehicle to review their current practices). It is also an opportunity to reflect on the workshop as a model for induction.

Point out the way in which the workshop has anatomised their current induction practice using the SharedThinking process. Highlight the shift from induction conceptualised as a series of presentations to an approach based on dialogue and interaction.

Highlight the theoretical aspects of the workshop as an alternative theory of induction which elaborates Tinto's ideas. You could also mention how this leads to a different view of learning design for induction. This theoretical approach is also one explanation of how the SharedThinking practice may work as a learning event.

This is a chance to ask if there are any questions or comments relating to either this workshop or any future events. Above all, make it clear that the processes and structures they have experienced in this workshop are identical to those used for student-generated induction elsewhere.

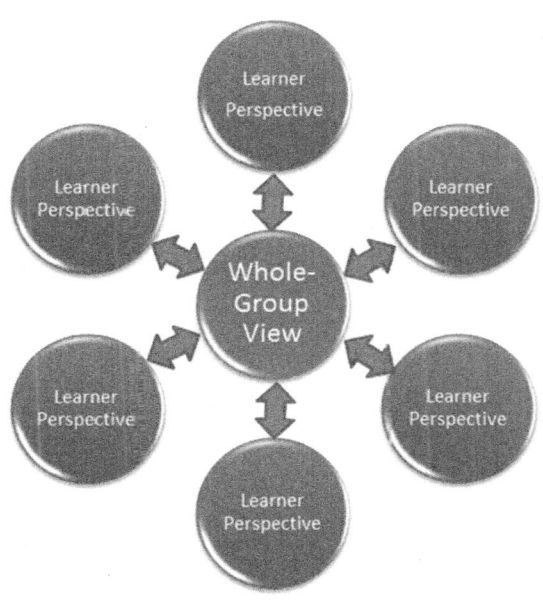

Part Four:

THE WORKSHOP SCRIPT

WORKSHOP: STUDENT-GENERATED INDUCTION: A SOCIAL IDENTITY APPROACH

Workshop Script

This script accompanies the slides that follow. Together they cover the presentations and the activity-structure for this workshop. You can use this script exactly as it stands using the same words. More likely, you may prefer to read the given script and adapt it to suit your needs.

Title Slide (Slide One)

Welcome to this workshop we are calling 'Student-Generated Induction: A Social Identity Approach.' The first part of the title is to do with the practice. The second part of it is to do with the theory.

We're glad you could come today and I hope that, above all, this will be an enjoyable and productive day for each of you.

This may be a good moment to tell participants about fire and safety regulations

You may also use the opportunity to tell participants about the nearest toilet facilities

The plan is that we will have two breaks for refreshments. That will be one in the morning and another in the afternoon. In between, there will be a lunch break as well. We should be due to finish at about 3.30 p.m.

Slide Two

Leaving aside the breaks for drinks and lunch, this is the structure of our day together. The aim is to make this as conversational as possible and to facilitate a discussion amongst you about your practices, experiences and thoughts as they relate to induction.

As we do so, we'll also be modelling the student-generated approach we've developed as one application of the SharedThinking practice. What you'll experience in this workshop is the same process the students experienced for their induction in various UK universities.

So, in the morning we'll be exploring your concerns and your success stories to do with induction. We will also be looking at the effects of using technology in the classroom for induction.

After lunch, we'll explore your concerns about induction and diversity as another issue to be addressed for induction and transition. We will then look at the theory and practice of the student-generated approach. That will take us on to explore different ways we might measure this different approach to induction.

We'll look at the theory in two parts. I'll say something about it in this introduction shortly and then I'll say a bit more about it in the afternoon. The idea is that by the end of the day you should at least have an idea about the theory and how it works in relation to the SharedThinking practice. So, let's get started with the introduction which will take about ten to fifteen minutes.

Slide Three

Vincent Tinto may be familiar to some of you as the person most referenced in the literature on induction and first year experience. Rather than trying to pull together literature from all over the place I thought I'd use Tinto as representative of the literature.

Tinto's theory is that we are more likely to retain students if we *integrate* them. This can refer to socialization into the university and its staff and students. It also refers to socialisation into the discipline which happens via the course.

Tinto promotes the idea that we should encourage a greater sense of belonging. I suggest that might equate to identification with the institution, at some level. This is because when we identify we often feel a sense of belonging. The focus of our identification becomes part of who we are as a member of that institution.

To develop this further, Tinto also suggests that we might achieve this sense of belonging by developing students in learning communities. This is seen as a way to promote both academic and social integration.

The issue then becomes how to define a learning community. What does it mean for us in this context? Even if we can define it, we also have to frame the learning community to know who is involved and who we are leaving out of the community. Is it to be framed at the course, the faculty or the university, for example?

We need to know this because the way we conceptualise our notional community will influence the way we go about designing and then implementing our practice for induction. This is part of what we're going to look at today in this workshop. Today is about an exploration of these ideas so that we can support induction, transition and retention.

Slide Four

As a way into this here are some different ways we could think about the design task for induction. There are three possible ways in which we might look at this. They are at an individual level, a structural level or we can base it on identity—specifically social identity.

It is important to say that although I'm favoring the one on social identity today, for the purpose of this workshop, I am certainly not suggesting that any one of these three approaches is better than any other. The first two of these are important and still need to be considered. I am drawing attention to the social identity approach because it is a different way of thinking and designing induction which has seldom been considered – until now.

Slide Five

The first of these three design approaches is the individual level of induction. This is the idea that the boundaries of a successful induction are largely a matter of what goes on in the learners mind. In practical terms, this involves the designer picturing a representative individual and thinking about what they may already know. To this is added the information they need to know on their arrival at the university.

Once we have done that, we then need to organize the information in the way that best helps that notional individual to receive it and to process it in their minds. At that point, it's the job of the individual to make sense of the information in their own context and to act upon it in an appropriate way. So, this is a view of induction based on a sense of individual responsibility and it's a design approach that regards the issue as being mainly within the boundaries of the individual mind.

Slide Six

Another way we can look at the design of induction is at the structural level. Here we might think about the way in which we organize the support services. This includes the people the students need to know about. It includes the way we market those services. It would also include telling them about some of the resources we have to offer and different ways students might access them.

Under this heading, we could also consider the ways in which we organize our activities in the electronic environment. So, we might think about having a page on Facebook or offering podcasts, email alerts, and web pages.

The point is that this can be seen as a structural view of the way we organize and support induction. The individual and the structural levels are both important and they need to be considered. Even so, there's also another way we could look at it.

Slide Seven

So, the other way of thinking about induction and transition is based on identity—and specifically on social identity. The important point I am trying to get across here is that this is a significant move away from thinking about induction at the individual level or the structural level. Even so, there are aspects of both involved in this idea of a social identity approach.

We could say that this kind of approach is not so much student-centred but group-centred. It's an approach to induction based upon who we are as a group and as members of different groups. So, let me say a bit more about that to clarify and explain what I mean.

Slide Eight

Firstly, we need to distinguish between personal identities and social identities. Personal identities could be thought of as our individual quirks or idiosyncrasies. They are the things that make us different from everyone else.

We also need to say just what we mean when we talk about social identities. You can see just some examples here. There are very many more too. Specifically, social identities have to do with the sense of ourselves as members of a particular group. We are members of a range of different groups as part of our profile.

More importantly, and following on from what I mentioned before, a social identity is not something contained within the boundaries of the individual mind. These are identities that others have as well.

For example, I might see myself as a footballer but if I did then I wouldn't be the only person with that identity. If that was the case, and I was the only one with that identity, then it wouldn't be possible to have a game of football and to organize ourselves to play on a pitch for ninety minutes. It wouldn't be possible to have a game of two halves and for each team to play together. This requires a shared understanding of how football is played. So, as Alex Haslam suggests, these social identities are a way of coordinating our actions around a shared view of the world.

We have many social identities and they have different levels of significance for each person sharing them. So I might have an obsessive interest in football, you might have a mild interest and this other person could be somewhere in the middle. It's different for each of us.

Even if everyone in this room happened to share a love of football that social identity would also be less likely to be active in this setting. Football has very little to do with a workshop on induction so it's doubtful that it would be an activated identity in our minds. This is even if we're interested in football and we identify with that sport. However, if we all hopped on a train and went to Wembley Stadium to watch a cup final then it might be different. Then it is more likely to be an active social identity in each of our minds. So, from this, we can say that social identities are context-sensitive at the level of the individual and they are also context-sensitive in the situational sense.

Slide Nine

What we can certainly say is that our social identities are to do with the way we see ourselves as members of different groups. When we identify with a group, we see it as part of who we are and we belong to that group. In the context of induction, we are trying to develop this sense of membership – a sense of belonging to the group and, by extension, to the institution.

It's also worth considering the other side of this to understand the implications of failure. When we become socially isolated there may be serious consequences for our health and well-being.

For some people, particularly the elderly, social isolation can be more harmful than cigarettes and alcohol. Alex Haslam's work has suggested that social isolation can lead to clinical depression and decreased memory function for example.

In the context of induction and transition, it is important to understand that groups are not just ways of structuring interaction and providing different ways of learning something. When we identify with a group, its norms are likely to influence our feelings, our thoughts and our behavior (Haslam, Eggins et al. 2003). This is at the heart of our interest in social identity theory for learning.

Slide Ten

So, in order to make this theory and this idea of influence into something more concrete, here is an interesting quote that came out of an interview done with a second year student. We asked about their experience as they arrived at the university a year earlier. I have to say this was quite a revelation to me in some ways because it suggests there are implications here for different stakeholders. I'll let you read it for a moment.

Note: we have found workshop participants often recognise and acknowledge this quote as fairly representative. It is worth pausing to explicitly ask whether or not they believe this quote has any wider truth in their experience.

As providers of induction and support services, this suggests that you may have a wonderful service filled with marvellous professionals, just like yourselves, but that may not be enough. You might also have pages on Facebook and a helpdesk staffed with people speaking several languages. However, if the students are most influenced by their peers then you could potentially be wasting a lot of time and money.

Equally, the students may not get help they may actually need. If they follow their perceptions of their peers, with whom they identify even before they meet, they may avoid important sources of help.

So, we're not saying those other levels of design are unimportant. They are very much worthwhile and necessary. I *am* saying that there are other issues that we may have overlooked and these may have important consequences.

Slide Eleven

So, it's based on this idea of working at the group and social identity level that we've developed a practice called SharedThinking. This is a scalable practice. For instance, we've used this approach with groups of over three hundred students in a single induction session. We've used it for transition as well and you'll have a chance to experience this, at least in its most basic form, during this workshop.

Slide Twelve

Having said all that, this final slide is meant as a way to clarify what we mean by the term 'student-generated induction.' This is a process which is in marked contrast to induction as a series of presentations, like this. It's also a process that includes the feelings, as much as the thoughts, of those involved. We don't separate out information-giving from emotional responses and support. Feelings are important in student-generated induction. It's about the whole person as well as the group.

As a provider of student-generated induction, this is also very much about facilitating a conversation to do with the concerns and interests of peers. In that respect, what they have to say to each other is at least as important as the things we have to say to them. Our relationship to the group becomes one of supporting and supplementing their conversations with the things they *couldn't* know about. It's the idea of induction and support coming from within the group. This is a long way from the idea of us *telling* them what we think they need to know.

This is a social and participatory approach to induction. Here, the term 'social' is about the students mixing with each other and each individual is involved with others. It also relates to the development of a social group. There is a collective sense of the social in this approach and that whole-group has a level of agency in the process.

Developing a sense of ownership is very much a feature of this approach to induction. The knowledge and experience within the group is central to this induction process. It is not dependent upon external knowledge although the staff perspective remains important. Through their interaction and dialogue, the students should develop a sense of who they are as a group.

All these aims are supported through the use of classroom technologies. These include the use of voting technologies and we'll be having a go with that, in a moment. For larger groups, we've used interactive whiteboards and a slightly modified structure.

Finally, I want to bring this full circle back to Tinto. I would suggest that student-generated induction and the SharedThinking practice is perhaps less vague than the idea of a learning community. Instead, we are talking about a specific group in a particular situation. In this approach, because it is so concrete, you can probably point to the people involved. We are clear about who is involved.

That's probably enough of me—or even too much—so let's change the dynamic. From here on, we're going to shift into the participative mode to reflect the student-generated approach to induction.

As preparation for this, we're going to start off by getting comfortable with the technology. We also want to use this opportunity to make sure it works!

Note that the next three slides require you to develop some general knowledge questions. At this point you will also require the use of voting technologies sometimes called clickers or audience response systems.

Slide Thirteen

So now we'll do the technology warm up. I've been raiding the pub quiz web site for you and this will allow us to test that the technology works and also to help you feel more comfortable before we use it for the real activities to follow.

Slide Fourteen

Note: Create and use your own choice of question here. Read your question and the options the participants should consider before they vote. Invite them to vote and tell them the right answer after the pie-chart is generated.

So the first question is:

Would you please vote now?

Slide Fifteen

Note: Create and use your own choice of question here. Read your question and the options the participants should consider before they vote. Invite them to vote and then tell them the right answer after the pie-chart is generated.

So the second question is:

Would you please vote now?

Slide Sixteen

Note: Create and use your own choice of question here. Read your question and the options the participants should consider before they vote. Invite them to vote and then tell them the right answer after the pie-chart is generated.

So the third question is:

Would you please vote now?

We've tested the technology and we know it works. You all seem to be quite comfortable using the handsets to vote so we are ready to begin the more serious work that follows. We're going to take a short break for coffee and then we'll get started.

This is also a good point for a short tea break if it feels appropriate. Otherwise, carry straight on with the next slide.

Slide Seventeen

I hope you are all feeling refreshed. Now, with your consent, we're going to have a go at the SharedThinking approach as it was used in the very first student-generated induction session.

I'm going to ask you to start by working on your own for two minutes. Would you each write down the main concern you have about your current induction practice?

Allow a couple of minutes to pass so each person has enough time to write down their view of the issue

Now, would you all share what you've written down with the rest of your table/small groups and, as a group, please can you come up with one issue you think the rest of the class should know about? Can you please appoint a spokesperson to report back and we'll give you fifteen minutes for that task.

Allow a period of fifteen to twenty minutes for participants to work in small groups.

Walk around the groups and pause to listen to the nature of the conversations before asking the groups if they have identified a single issue they are ready to share. You may need to do this twice with an interval between.

So, please can we come together as a class again and hear what each group has chosen? Can we begin with the group at the back? What did you decide and can you tell us why? Thank you for that. What about that next group? What did you come up with and why?...That's interesting....and the next table?

Ask each group and gather their feedback. Verify their response and offer a comment where appropriate. Record each group's feedback as an option on the screen.

Here is the set of options that have come out of the discussions you've all had in your groups. Would you each pick up your handset and vote for the issue you think is most important? That means select the issue which is most important to you individually, regardless of your group's choice.

Activate the software to be able to receive the votes and allow them time to make their decisions using the handsets.

Here is the pie chart which summarises your views on what concerns you most about your current induction practice.

Make any brief comments and acknowledge the voting outcomes. Pick up any significant points and allow any further comments from the participants. Then move on quickly enough to restore the focus back to the process.

Slide Eighteen

I thought you might be interested in seeing the outcome of the same process delivered for student-generated induction. In other words, this is what the students were actually concerned about as they arrived at university.

Show the example pie-chart from the online resource collection

There are a number of points to say about this.

1. Firstly, we should be aware that what's really important here is that the students are telling each other these things. It's easy to get into the mind-set that this is about them telling you—which they are—but it's also very much about them establishing the common ground that exists amongst these students-as-strangers who have just walked into the university together.

2. Unlike the conventional use of this technology, all the issues are important or correct. So, something that got no votes is just as important as another issue which attracted more votes. The reason is because these were all issues raised and agreed in the small groups. They were valued enough to be shared with the rest of the class so they need a response.

3. Looking at the pie-chart, you can see the influence happening as the issues raised in small groups are abandoned when they came to the voting. That's because each small group influences other small groups and because individually they are free to vote as they wish regardless of their group. Each person can use the group as a resource.

4. It does also communicate to you and, even though you could have predicted some of these things, your response to these issues tells the students you're listening. This is heightened because, through the student-generated pie-chart, you are able to provide a socially-contingent response. As you can imagine, this is better than just telling them what you think they need to know.

Slide Nineteen

In this next activity, we are going to look at the other side of your practice. This time we're going to ask you to think about something that really worked well in your induction practice. With your consent, we'll explore the positive side of your practice using a similar process to the one we used before. However, this time we're going to do it without the technology. When we've done that, we'll compare these two activities to understand the effect of the technology upon this kind of activity structure.

So, if you were a reporter in the last group activity would you please change tables? Would you please not be the reporter this next time?

Can you please begin by working on your own again? Please write down something you'd see as a positive aspect of your current induction practice? We'll give you a couple of minutes to write something down and then we'll go into groups for a discussion.

Allow a couple of minutes for everyone to write down their item to be shared in their groups.

Have you all got something written down? Good! Would you please work in your groups and share what you've written down and say why you chose that point? Then, in your small groups, can you come up with one point that you think is most useful to share with the rest of us? We'll give you fifteen to twenty minutes to do that.

Allow a period of fifteen to twenty minutes for participants to work in small groups. Walk around the groups and pause to listen to the nature of the conversations before asking the groups if they have identified a single issue they are ready to share. You may need to do this twice with an interval between.

Let's go to the right side of the room this time and ask what you've put. What about the next group? What did you come up with...That's good...and the next table?

[Using a flip chart and marker pen, write down the decisions of each small group. Carry on until you have recorded all the groups' options].

Now we've got them all recorded can we have a show of hands for who thinks the first one is the most significant. And how many think the second option is the one to highlight most? ....

[*Count the votes for each option and write them down on the flipchart. Carry on until participants have voted on all of the options*]

Here we have the votes for each option on our flipchart. This allows us to see the variety of positive aspects of your practice and it shows the collective-view of those ideas.

Slide Twenty

In the first activity, we explored the concerns you had about your current induction practice. We did that using a particular structure to help organise this group discussion. In addition, we also used the voting technology. That was the most basic SharedThinking approach.

In the second activity, we explored the positive aspects of your current induction practice. We still used the same activity-structure but this time we did it without the use of the technology. In that case we used the flipchart and pens instead. We then voted by a show of hands.

Slide Twenty-One

Your activity now is to work in your groups for about ten minutes and to think about the difference between those two activities we've just done. Specifically, what difference did the technology make between the first and the second activity?

To help you with this task, we've outlined some of the headings you might use to organize your response. So, when you do this comparison, you might ask what difference the two approaches made in terms of the outcomes, the process, the feelings it generated, and any other categories you can think of together. You might also have some other things that struck you as different and more important. There is no need to stick to these outcomes if they don't fit with your experience. They are just there to help get you started with your thinking.

I'll give you ten minutes to see what you can come up with. Then we'll come back together to see what we've got.

[*Allow the groups enough time to reflect and discuss the issues and to feed-back to the class. Alternatively, you can run this as a plenary without small group work.*]

It's probably fair to say that it is quicker to do this using the technology. We get a clearer picture of the group-view with the technology and we also get pretty close to a 100% response compared with the hand-raising approach. We can also do different things with the pie-charts as an artifact. These things are more problematic using a show of hands and counting up for each option. You can imagine what that might be like in a larger group as well. That's enough to think about for now.

Slide Twenty-Two

This morning, we began by looking at Tinto's idea of retention and integration. We looked at Tinto's suggestion that learning communities could be a solution. We then looked at three levels of induction design before going on to talk about social iden-tity as an alternative theory and design strategy. This was an approach based upon *groups* rather than communities.

We followed this up and used the student-generated approach with and with-out technology. That allowed us to explore the impact of the technology within the same activity structure. This afternoon, we'll develop this by looking at the theory in more depth and different ways we might measure this approach. For now...

Slide Twenty-Three

Lunch Time

Slide Twenty-Four

Welcome back everyone. So just to re-cap, this morning we used the basic Shared-Thinking process to share concerns about your induction practice. We then looked at the positive aspects of your practice without the technology. That took us into a consideration of two key design elements of student-generated induction—the discussion structure and the technology.

This afternoon we want to try and develop that a bit further by looking at the theory behind the student-generated approach. Specifically, we want to look at how the SharedThinking process might work in that theoretical framework.

We also began the day looking at the different ways we can think about the design of induction from the individual point of view, the structural view or the social identity perspective. I want to build upon that earlier introduction to say more about the theory so you can get a better explanation of the practice.

Slide Twenty-Five

Even though this relates to theory, we're still keen to keep this relevant to the topic of induction. We still want it to be situated within a conversation about your own practice. We still want it to be social and participative.

Before we begin, if you were a reporter in the last group activity would you please change tables? Would you please not be the reporter this next time?

This next activity should connect nicely into an overview of the theory. I also hope it will be a useful and important issue to discuss anyway. I'd like to ask you, starting with writing on your own, what is your main concern about addressing diversity at induction?

Allow the participants a couple of minutes to write something down.

Now, would you please share those issues you've written down with your small group? Again, could each group choose one issue to share with the rest of the class? We'll give you fifteen minutes to discuss that and then we'll ask for some feedback. Away you go.

Allow a period of fifteen to twenty minutes for participants to work in small groups. Walk around the groups and pause to listen to the nature of the conversations before asking the groups if they have identified a single issue they are ready to share. You may need to do this twice with an interval between.

So, please can we come together as a class again and hear what each group has chosen? Can we begin with this group on the left? What did you decide and can you tell us why? Thank you for that. What about that next group? What did you come up with and why?...That's interesting....and the next table?

Ask each group and gather their feedback. Verify their response and offer a comment where appropriate. Record each group's feedback as an option on the screen.

Here is the set of options that have come out of the discussions you've all had in your groups. Would you each pick up your handset and vote for the issue you think is most important? That means select the issue which is most important to you individually, regardless of your group's choice.

Thank you for that and I hope that was useful in itself. This time I'm not going to dwell on the particular issues because I want to make the connection to the theory.

Slide Twenty-Six

Let me join some theoretical dots here. We could argue that diversity poses a challenge which is to provide education in a socially sensitive way. On the one hand, we very much want to value, respect and support diversity. These are all the things that enrich our lives and help our learning. On the other hand, we have the additional goal, put forward by Tinto, to integrate the new arrivals into a unified learning community. Are these different goals at odds with each other? How might they be reconciled?

The good news is that we may not need to choose between them! We may be able to do both. It need not be an 'either or' situation. And in fact, we can think about social diversity as social identities. Race, religion, ethnicity etc. are all examples of social identities.

We sometimes also think about diversity as something fixed. We risk thinking about people in that one way. Instead, we can see identity as fluid and context-sensitive rather than as something fixed across all settings. That way, we can look at the world through different lenses according to the particular needs and depending on each situation. This helps in theory and practice for induction. I will explain what I mean.

In developing student-generated induction, we used Social Identity Theory from social psychology. This theory says that at any given moment our identity lies somewhere along this continuum (Tajfel, 1974). At one end we see ourselves as distinct from any group. This is our personal identity and 'who I am.'

At the other end of the continuum, I may think of myself as a member of a group. In fact, this could be any one of several groups of which we may be a member. At this point, we might talk about ourselves as who 'we' are. At such a moment, I don't distinguish myself from other members of the group. When that social identity is engaged, I am a member of the group like any other. I am de-personalised.

Slide Twenty-Seven

When my particular social identity is activated, and we all have many social categories, we identify with that group and favour it over other groups. We get one of those 'Us' and 'Them' situations.

For example, if I see myself as a fan of one football team then I will favour my team. At the same time I will disfavour another team and their fans. According to Henri Tajfel's theory this is known as 'Ingroup Bias.'

When students arrive at a university they may have any one of their social identities activated in their own minds. Equally, they may have a social identity activated by their perception of the social context. We have this social diversity in action. Put another way, this is a situation in which many social identities may be active in the room.

Your task is to get them all engaged with thinking about their arrival at university, even if only for a while. Theoretically, this is the task of getting them to each have the same social identity activated at the same time.

Slide Twenty-Eight

One way to break down these psychological boundaries between one identity and another is to invoke a different higher level identity—a super ordinate category (Haslam, Eggins et al. 2003). Identities are fluid so if it doesn't work, the students will probably return to their sub-group identities being active.

The invoked category needs to be important to the participants for it to have a chance of holding. The key is to support inter-group dialogue and to help them co-construct the unifying identity.

Let me give you another example. If I arrive at university seeing myself as a member of the working class and I perceive everyone else in the room to be upper class then it may heighten and activate my working class identity. However, if I suddenly find out that some of them are also keen on football and they also invited me to go and see the game then suddenly my working class social identity may be deactivated. In that moment, we're all part of a group called football fans. We've effectively neutralised the inter-group tensions by changing the salient identity. We have changed the active identity away from social class to football.

Slide Twenty-Nine

To give you a case study from our induction practice, we put three hundred students through a SharedThinking process. More importantly, we addressed this at the faculty level.

This involved students from Psychology, Computing Science and Mathematics. Through the SharedThinking process, the students created a view of the common ground between them. This was done in the same way as you did just now and also this morning.

By doing that, we were prompting the students to think not about their discipline-identity but about being students in this university. They changed the active social identity by co-constructing a new one for a particular situation.

Importantly, this doesn't disallow their subject identity. It provides what's called a common ingroup identity (Gaertner, Dovidio et al. 1993), which is this other social category of 'being a student here.' It's also why we might think about diversity as a form of social identity. We can see this view of identity as something fluid.

So, that's the theory and one way it might address diversity at induction. We change the active identity for a purpose. It doesn't stop them being all those other things as well.

Slide Thirty

We also asked the students what they expected induction to be like—because we knew this was a different take on the conventional idea—and this is what one student said and the outcome of that change.

Read the quotes on the slide out loud or let the participants read it for themselves.

We can almost see these two quotes as 'before' and 'after' the student-generated approach was introduced. It is equally interesting to note that, just as you were concerned that your current practice seems to involve a lot of information-giving (based on the first activity of this workshop), so these students reflect those perceptions. They've been encultured to expect just that! The cultural norm for induction could be said to be information-giving and students as an audience.

The quote on the bottom of the slide is also interesting. If the theory is right then we'd expect students to feel as though they belonged to the group. That is just what we found. This student, as an example, moved from feeling like an outsider to feeling that they were on the inside—they felt as though they belonged. It also affected their feelings and addressed their social isolation. This person no longer felt alone. All of this is consistent with the theory.

Slide Thirty-One

Let me just try and pull this together again with a quick review. We started off this morning with Tinto's ideas of developing learning communities to improve retention. From there, we got onto the idea of social identity as a possible basis for designing induction. This is a collective approach based on developing a sense of who 'we' are as a class.

I'm suggesting that *groups* are more concrete and useful compared with communities. Maybe a sense of community is just a feeling of belonging to a group or a feeling that we identify with it. Is it a kind of group learning we're talking about here? Following on from that, and before we break for tea, I want to look at the issue of group-work in induction.

Slide Thirty-Two

We're going to do another run of the SharedThinking process, our basic student-generated approach to induction, and this time we're going to explore our concerns about group learning.

If you were a reporter last time would you please move to another table and can I ask that you don't be the reporter next time.

So, starting off individually, would you write down your main concern about using group learning for your induction practice?

Allow the participants a couple of minutes to write something down.

Now, would you please share those individual concerns with your small group? Again, could each group choose one to share with the rest of the class? We'll give you fifteen minutes to discuss that and then we'll ask for some feedback. Away you go.

Allow a period of fifteen to twenty minutes for participants to work in small groups. Walk around the groups and pause to listen to the nature of the conversations before asking the groups if they have identified a single issue they are ready to share. You may need to do this twice with an interval between.

So, please can we come together as a class again and hear what each group has chosen? Can we begin with this group at the front? What did you decide and can you tell us why? Thank you for that. What about that next group? What did you come up with and why?...That's interesting....and the next table?

Ask each group and gather their feedback. Verify their response and offer a comment where appropriate. Record each group's feedback as an option on the screen.

Here is the set of options that have come out of your group discussions. Would you each pick up your handset and vote for the issue you think is most important? That means select the issue which is most important to you individually, regardless of your group's choice.

Note: This is an opportunity to explore and respond to the issues raised. You might also invite the participants to consider how well the SharedThinking process they're using would address some of those concerns.

Aside from any responses I might make, to the particular points raised, your interaction provides me with a shape for my response. Hopefully, that would mean that my reply would be contingent with your conversation and your concerns.

This is also a way for the group to communicate. The pie-chart tells each individual member what 'we' think. This is the collective view on this issue. More importantly, it gives each of you an opportunity to compare your thoughts and feelings with those of the rest of the class. By making the discussion visible in this way, the group can serve as a resource for each person.

Remember that we are modelling the process we used the first time we delivered the student-generated induction approach. At that point, as they arrive on their first day, they believe all kinds of things about the institution, their peers and about themselves. They probably don't know that others feel the same. SharedThinking is as much about you talking to each other as it is about hearing anything I might add.

My role is to help supplement your conversations. In addition, I'm organising the view of the group. That's the view of the group on different issues and in relation to other issues and groups. I'll say more on that later.

Slide Thirty-Three

Let's break for tea. When we come back, we're going to look at some different ways we might measure student-generated induction. Thank you.

Allow about 15 minutes for a break

Slide Thirty-Four

Welcome back. You've worked hard and we're nearly at the end now. In this last activity, we thought it could be useful to look at measures we can use to look at student-generated induction.

There are several different measures available to you using this approach. However, it is important to be aware of the way that these measures can have as much value and utility for the students as for the staff.

Slide Thirty-Five

The first thing to say is that here we have a view of collective experience and it is created in a relatively short time—maybe a couple of hours. Remember this is a chart showing the issues within the group. It also shows their distribution across a whole-group at a given moment in time. Another important point is that it is very representative of the group because it reflects almost 100 per cent participation.

So this is an alternative to carrying out student surveys. Using conventional methods, it is quite rare to achieve 100 per cent feedback and it certainly takes a lot more time. That conventional approach typically uses questions set by the researcher. That can be fine but it may risk exploring issues that are not the main concern of the students. Here they are student-generated so we know they are reasonably socially-authentic.

This is also something that benefits the participants. They can trust it because this is data that has not left the room. It is not taken away to be analysed by someone before it is presented back to the class. They can trust the information because they created it and nobody tampered with it. They are co-researchers, if you like.

It is also a measure for the participants to gauge the social context in which they reside. It allows them to normalise, or at least to compare, their thinking relative to the rest of the class. It also does that for an issue that is relevant and important to everyone present. In this way, it gives each person a way of understanding the group norms on a particular issue and it supports the idea of the group as a learning resource for its members.

Slide Thirty-Six

For this activity, you can use two pie charts from other sessions. Those pie-charts should both address the same topic but generated by different groups. See the online resource base for examples you could use. You can prepare this before the workshop begins.

Alternatively, take the pie-chart generated by the workshop group in the last activity and place it alongside a pie-chart from the online resource base (or from another workshop group). If you choose this option, prepare it during the tea break.

Let me just develop this idea of measurement a bit further, if I may. We have on the left of the screen the chart you generated in the last activity. It covers the issues you had regarding the use of group learning for induction.

On the right hand side of the screen, you can see the views of another group of tutors on this very same issue. We ran exactly the same activity, in another institution, asking those tutors about their concerns regarding the use of group learning.

As a result of these different sessions, we are able to help a group understand their views in relation to other groups. By doing this kind of comparison we can help the group understand themselves in a wider context. In this case, you can compare two groups to see how typical or how different this group is on the issue of group learning.

As a workshop provider, I can do the same comparison. This can help me evaluate my practice in relation to other groups on the same issue. It can also help me understand my workshop group in greater depth.

I would like to invite you to do one more activity. Would you work in your groups and look at these two pie-charts. What do you think is the impact of seeing these two pie-charts together? What is the impact on you as participants and then as a provider? Would you just take ten minutes to look and we'll report back in an open session.

Allow ten minutes for a discussion in small groups.

Let's see what we've got. Anyone like to start?

Take any responses and comment on them. Allow other workshop participants to comment.

The main point I want to get across to you is that grouping these charts has possibilities for students and staff alike. They are pedagogical tools. In addition, we are able to do comparative measures at the collective level quickly and efficiently.

Slide Thirty-Seven

Another thing we can do is to measure collective change, for a single cohort of students, over time. Here is an example. On your left is our physiotherapy group as they arrived at university. We looked at this chart earlier on this morning if you remember. On the right is the same group a year further on in their studies.

We can use the SharedThinking approach to generate a chart for the entire journey of a course. This allows us to understand the way their needs change over time. It helps the students understand their achievement or their destiny. At the same time, it allows the facilitator to evaluate their course with different cohorts at the collective level.

Slide Thirty-Eight

Over the time we've been doing this, we've become aware of quite a few different ways you can measure and work with change at the collective level. One of them is the ability to measure the impact of inputs by tutors, mentors or support staff.

In another intervention, we ran a SharedThinking session with a group of new arrivals on the issue of making friends at university. We followed that by inviting some mentors to interact with them and for them to offer some advice to the newcomers.

We then repeated the vote on the same issues. The pie-charts show the level of influence the mentors had on these new students. The point is that we are able to measure impact of a particular intervention at that collective level.

Slide Thirty-Nine

We've had a long and quite intensive day. It is probably worth reviewing what we have done today. That will allow us to think about the value of the workshop and what we may have learned.

Slide Forty

We began with the aim of facilitating a discussion amongst you in a way that would allow you to share issues and ideas to do with your own induction practices. The aim was for the workshop to be useful as a reflective opportunity for you but also to introduce a new theory and practice for induction.

In doing this, we also sought to model the idea and the practice of student-generated induction. The aim was that this should be an experiential approach to help you consider the possibility of making changes in your practice. We used the basic student-generated induction approach in order to support your dialogue and interaction at different points in this workshop.

During the course of this workshop, we were able to explore a range of aspects of your induction practice. These related to concerns, positives, diversity, and group learning for induction.

At the same time, you were able to explore the design-variables in the design of student-generated induction. We compared design features in two activities which used the same activity-structure. This allowed us to consider some of the variables within the process. We saw some of the ways we could vary it.

We also looked at some theoretical issues. We considered a psychological or individual view of induction design. We looked at structural aspects of design. We then considered the idea of designing induction around social identity.

We also explored the practicalities of Tinto's idea that we should develop students in learning communities. We used social identity theory, and student-generated induction, to propose groups and group-learning as an alternative. This provided us with a more practical approach as well as a new theory of induction.

Finally, we looked at different ways of measuring a student-generated approach to induction. We considered the value of these measures for different stakeholders. We also noted different ways we could explore and use collective experience in practice as a pedagogical and evaluative tool.

Slide Forty-One

I think that's a fair bit to digest. It is certainly a lot of work so thank you for all your time, energy and input today. I hope you can take something away and relate it to your own context.

This workshop covered the basics of this student-generated approach. We will also plan to run other workshops to dig deeper into the design, theory, practice, and research using this approach. Until then, thank you for coming today and a safe journey home.

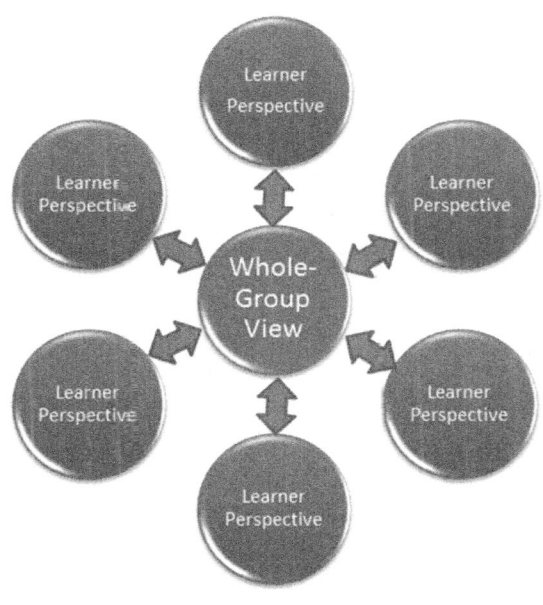

Part Five:

THE WORKSHOP SLIDES

WORKSHOP: STUDENT-GENERATED INDUCTION: A SOCIAL IDENTITY APPROACH

Workshop Slides

Slide One

Shared Thinking

Student-Generated Induction: A Social Identity Approach

Slide Two

Structure of the day

10.45 Introduction: Outline of the day, defining terms and background

11.00 Technology Warm Up

11.15 Coffee and tea break

11.30 Sharing Current Issues anc Concerns for Induction

12.00 Sharing success stories for induction

12.30 Learning Design for Studert—Generated Induction

12.45 LUNCH 1.15: Theory for Induction and Transition: Diversity and Incuction

2.00: Sharing Concerns using Group—Learning for Induction

2.30: TEA/COFFEE

2.45: Measures and Evaluation of Student—Generated Induction

3.15: Review

3.30: Close

Slide Three

Tinto and Induction

- Retention depends upon Integration

  - Socialisation into the institution

  - Socialisation into the discipline/course

  - Belonging (Identification)

- Strategies

  - Learning Communities

    - Definition?

    - Framing?

    - Implementation?

Tinto, V. (1995), "Learning communities, collaborative learning and the pedagogy of educational citizenship." AAHE Bulletin**47**: 11-13.

Tinto, V. (2000), "Learning better together: The impact of learning communities on student access in higher education." Journal of Institutional Research**9**(1): 48-53.

Slide Four

Learning Design for Induction

- Individual Level

- Structural Level

- Social Identity Level

Slide Five

Individual Level
Cognitive Processing

Induction as acquisition, assimilation, transfer, and needs

Slide Six

Structural Level
The Environment

Induction as organization of information, marketing, access and service

Slide Seven

Social Identity Level
Influence of Groups

Induction based on who *we* are as a group

(SharedThinking)

Slide Eight

Social Identities

A Sense of who we are as group members

Gender, race, ethnicities, clubs, sexuality, religion, social class, teams, political parties, regions, nationalities, hobbies, jobs, professions, student, academic, support professional, scientist, artist, physicist, psychologist, educator, musician, worker, family, first born, star sign, dancer, university,

Slide Nine

Groups and Membership

- Social Isolation is harmful (House)

- Possibly worse than smoking in some cases (House)

- Social Isolation impacts on cognition and language (Haslam)

- Groups are not just a passive structure (Haslam)

- Groups are an active influence on individual thought and behaviour (Haslam)

- Shared Identity - group norms as mediators

Slide Ten

Influence of Peers

"I didn't use that service because I didn't think any of the others in my year would." (Student)

Slide Eleven

SharedThinking

A **practice for a social identity approach**
already applied to induction and transition

Slide Twelve

Student-Generated Induction

- A contrast with a series of presentations

- As much about feelings as thoughts and facts

- As much about talking to peers as to tutors and support staff

- Agenda is owned and co-authored by participants

- Invoking a shared sense of group identity (who *we* are)

- Uses classroom technologies

- More concrete than *communities*

- Group-specific

Slide Thirteen

Slide Fourteen

General Knowledge Question 1

1. Type Option Here

2. Type Option Here

3. Type Option Here

4. Type Option Here

Slide Fifiteen

General Knowledge Question 2

1. Type Option Here

2. Type Option Here

3. Type Option Here

4. Type Option Here

Slide Sixteen

General Knowledge Question 3

1. Type Option Here

2. Type Option Here

3. Type Option Here

4. Type Option Here

Slide Seventeen

What is your main concern to do with your current induction practice?

1. Type Option Here

2. Type Option Here

3. Type Option Here

4. Type Option Here

5. Type Option Here

Slide Eighteen

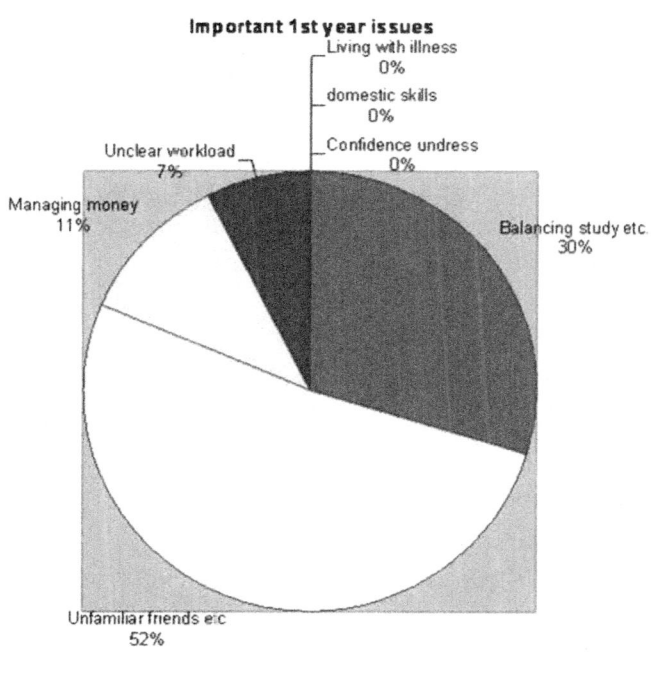

Slide Nineteen

What is the most positive thing to do with your current induction practice?

1. Type Option Here

2. Type Option Here

3. Type Option Here

4. Type Option Here

Slide Twenty

Design Elements

Review of Activities 1 and 2: The Impact of Technology

Slide Twenty One

The Impact of Technology

What difference did the technology make between activities 1 and 2?

- Participant Experience

- Process

- Outcomes

- Feelings

- Ownership

- Togetherness

Slide Twenty Two

Review of the Morning

- We looked at Tinto's theory and learning communities

- We looked at three ways we could design induction (Individual, Structural, **Social Identity**)

- Used Student-Generated approach to look at concerns with current induction practice

- Looked at positive aspects of current practice but without the technology

- Compared and contrasted to understand design elements in student-generated approach

Slide Twenty Three

Lunch Time!

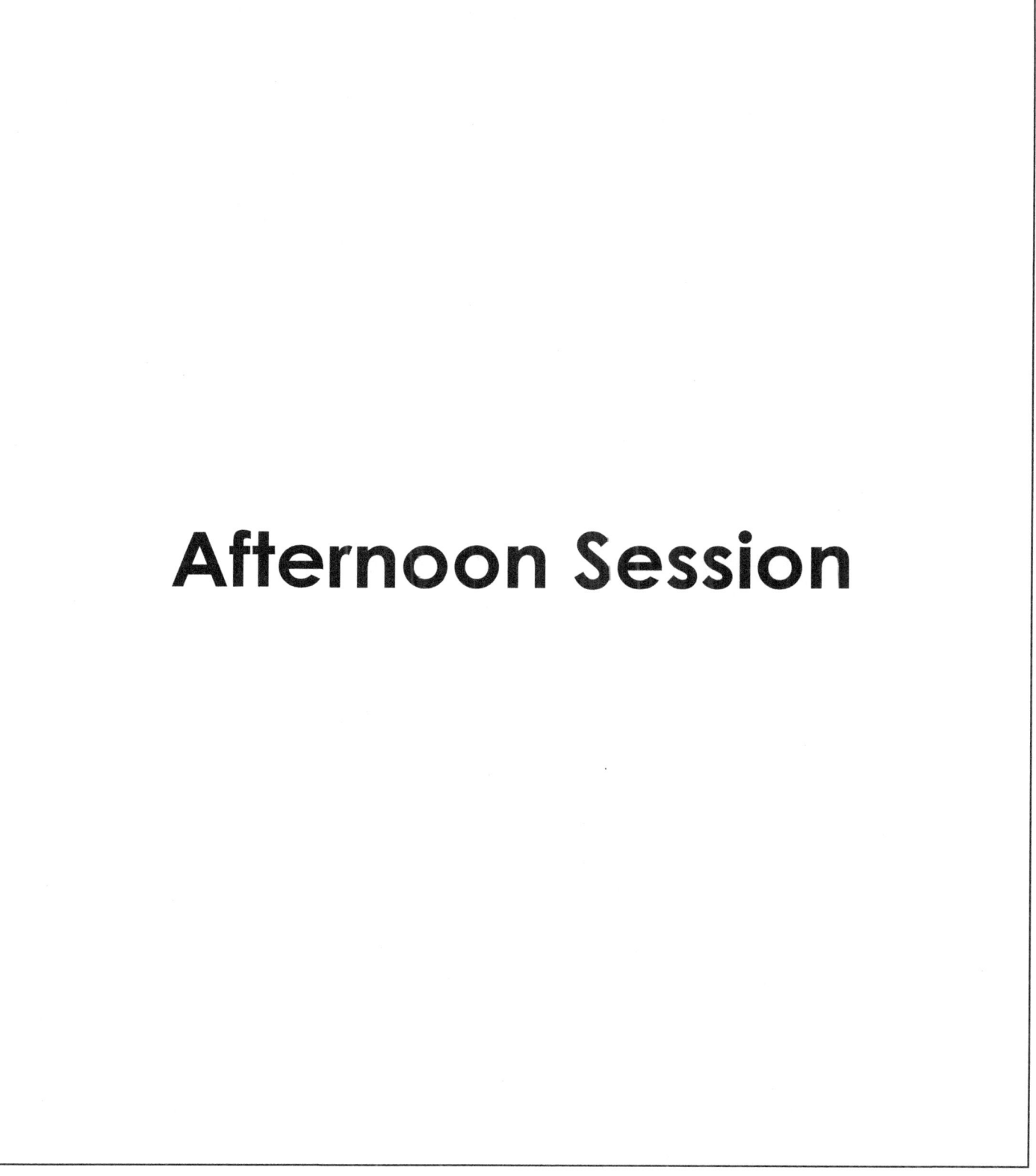

Afternoon Session

Slide Twenty Four

Slide Twenty Five

What is your main concern about addressing diversity at induction?

1. Type Option Here

2. Type Option Here

3. Type Option Here

4. Type Option Here

Slide Twenty Six

Social Identity Theory
(Tajfel)

Identity Continuum
(context-sensitive)

Me $\longleftrightarrow$ We

Slide Twenty Seven

Social Identity Theory

Ingroup bias (Tajfel)

Us   Them

Slide Twenty Eight

Social Identity Theory
(Turner)

Both of Us

Superordinate
Group/Identity
(Gaertner & Dovidio)

Subordinate
Group/Identity

Us   Them

Slide Twenty Nine

FIMS FACULTY CASE STUDY

Being a Student Here

Superordinate Group/Identity

Subordinate Group/Identity

Maths   **Comp. Science**   **Psychology**

Slide Thirty

Student Expectations of Induction

"Well I first thought…the lecturers, or whoever would be in charge, would just be talking then we would leave. Then I would expect other students to be there and they would give their opinions and then it would be questions and answers…[I was] more relieved that it wasn't just the standard hello goodbye and actually more welcoming and rather than just being talked to." [1st year student]

"…it made you feel less of an outsider and it made you feel a bit better that you're not just on your own." [1st year student]

Slide Thirty One

Learning Communities or Groups?

Slide Thirty Two

What is your main concern about using group learning for induction?

1. Type Option Here

2. Type Option Here

3. Type Option Here

4. Type Option Here

5. Type Option Here

Slide Thirty Three

Tea Time!

Slide Thirty Four

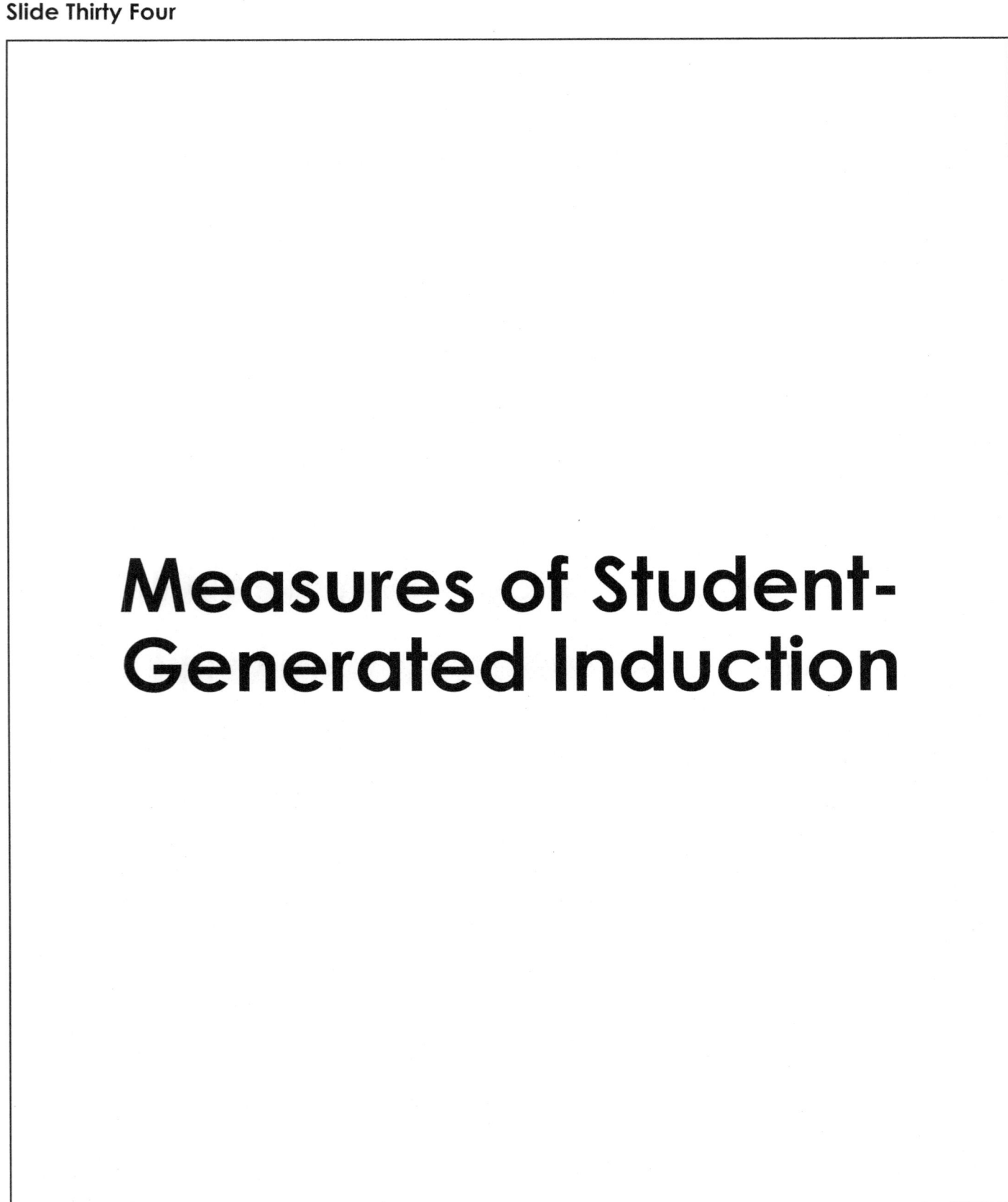

Measures of Student-Generated Induction

Slide Thirty Five

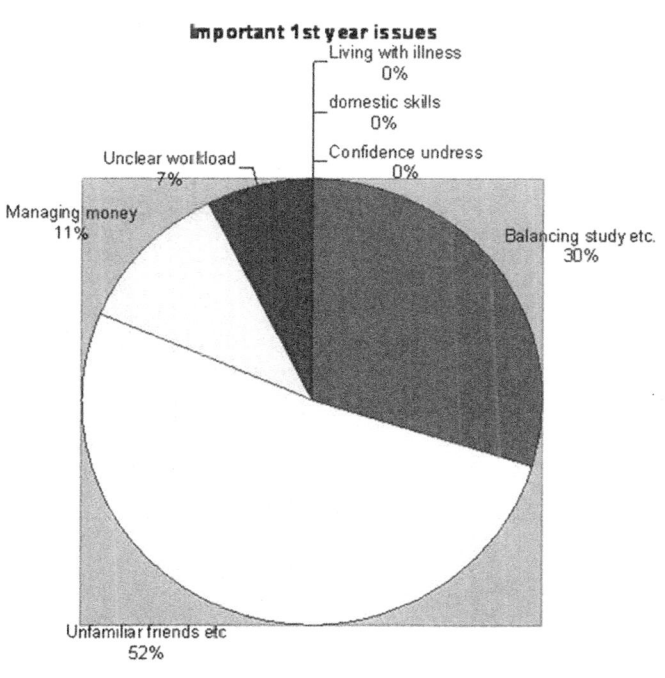

Measures of Collective Experience

Important 1st year issues

Slide Thirty Six

Comparative Measures

Us

1. Group size
2. Group Dynamics
3. Consistency of experience
4. Disengagement
5. Group Formation
6. Facilitation

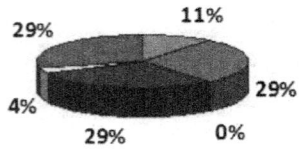

Them

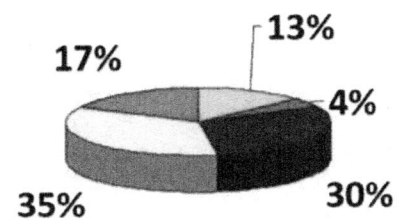

☐ Real time adaptation of the system
▨ Balanced input from all participants
■ Effective and efficient facilitation of groups
☐ A coherent experience and outcome
▨ Overcoming resistance and fear (of things that could go wrong) for students

Slide Thirty Seven

Other applications of comparative data at the collective level?

Start Year 1

Important 1st year issues

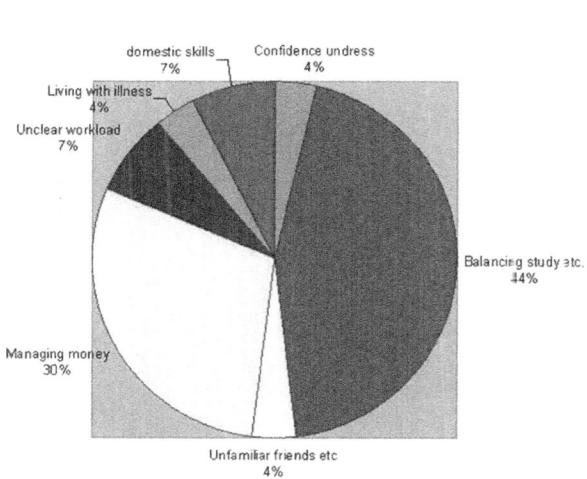

Living with illness 0%

domestic skills 0%

Confidence undress 0%

Unclear workload 7%

Managing money 11%

Balancing study etc. 30%

Unfamiliar friends etc 52%

Start Year 2

Issues that remain in year 2

domestic skills 7%

Confidence undress 4%

Living with illness 4%

Unclear workload 7%

Balancing study etc. 44%

Managing money 30%

Unfamiliar friends etc 4%

Slide Thirty Eight

Measuring Impact/Influence

Before

After

Making Friends Vote 1

Making Friends Vote 2

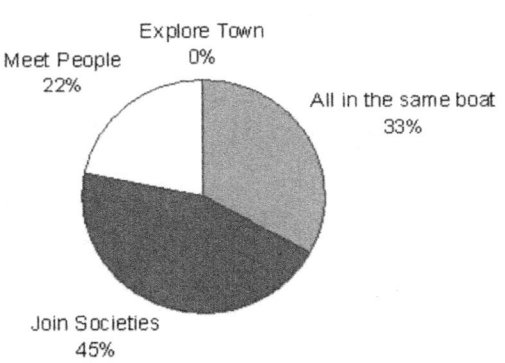

Slide Thirty Nine

Closing Review

What have we learned?

Slide Forty

We did this today

- Reviewed the concerns and positives in our current practice

- Compared design features of student-generated induction

- Looked at some theoretical aspects

- Looked at group-work for induction

- Looked at measures of student-generated induction

Slide Forty One

Thank You
Safe Journey Home

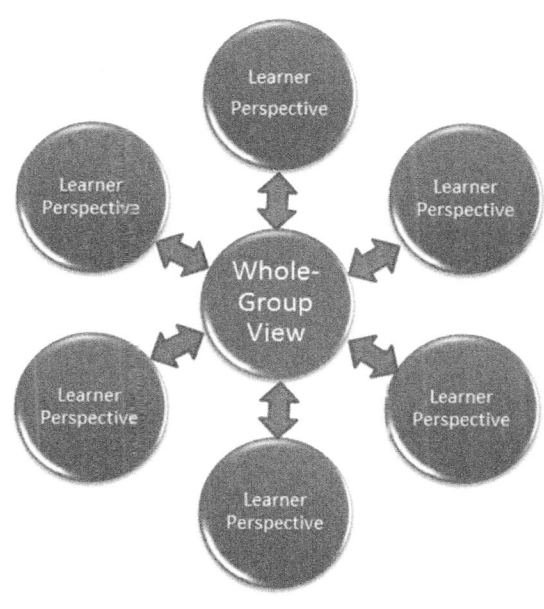

Part Six:

THE WORKSHOP READING LIST

STUDENT-GENERATED INDUCTION: A SOCIAL IDENTITY APPROACH

Workshop Reading List

Gaertner, S. L., J. F. Dovidio, et al. (1993). "The Common Ingroup Identity Model: Recategorization and the Reduction of Intergroup Bias." European Review of Social Psychology 4(1): 1-26.

Haslam, S. A., R. A. Eggins, et al. (2003). "The ASPIRe model: Actualizing Social and Personal Identity Resources to enhance organizational outcomes." Journal of Occupational and Organizational Psychology 76(1): 83-113.

Livingstone, A. G., S. A. Haslam, et al. (2011). ""We Are, Therefore We Should": Evidence That In-Group Identification Mediates the Acquisition of In-Group Norms." Journal of Applied Social Psychology 41(8): 1857-1876.

Moscovici, S. (1988). "Notes towards a description of Social Representations." European Journal of Social Psychology 18(3): 211-250.

Moscovici, S. and I. Markova (1998). "Presenting Social Representations: A Conversation." Culture Psychology 4(3): 371-410.

Piaget, J. (1977). Problems of equilibration Topics in cognitive development. M. H. Appel and L. S. Goldberg. New York, Plenum: 3-14.

Piaget, J. and B. Inhelder (1969). The Psychology of the child. New York, Basic Books, Inc.

Tajfel, H. (1969). "Cognitive aspects of prejudice." Journal of Social Issues 25: 79-97.

Tajfel, H. (1974). "Social identity and intergroup behaviour." Social Sciences Information/Information sur les Sciences Sociales 13: 65-93.

Thompson, L. and G. A. Fine (1999). "Socially shared cognition, affect, and behavior: a review and integration." Pers Soc Psychol Rev 3(4): 278-302.

Tinto, V. (1995). "Learning communities, collaborative learning and the pedagogy of educational citizenship." AAHE Bulletin 47: 11-13.

Tinto, V. (2000). "Learning better together: The impact of learning communities on student access in higher education." Journal of Institutional Research 9(1): 48-53.

Turner, J. C. (1975). "Social comparison and social identity: Some prospects for intergroup behaviour." European Journal of Social Psychology 5(1): 1-34.

Turner, J. C. (1991). Social Influence. Milton Keynes, Open University Press.

Vygotsky, L. S. (1978). Mind in Society: The development of higher psychological processes. Cambridge, MA, Harvard University Press.

Printed in Great Britain
by Amazon